Discovering
GOD'S
Sufficiency

Books by John F. Gillette:

Discovering God's Sufficiency
Going Beyond Ourselves and Experiencing the Supernatural
Pastoral Health Care — Part One

Discovering God's Love
Confirming God's love through the evidence of historical facts
Pastoral Health Care — Part Two

Discovering God's Counsel
Applying his spiritual solution to meet difficult trials
Pastoral Health Care — Part Three

Discovering God's Kingdom
Finding a way to understand ourselves in a complex world
Pastoral Health Care — Part Four

Discovering God's Heart
Feeling God's heart pulse is our daily challenge
Pastoral Health Care —Part Five

Glorify God
Christianity is a divine vitality
Divine Dialogue — Part One

Dynamic Doer
Biblical Christianity is Jesus Christ
Divine Dialogue — Part Two

Spiritual Solutions
Union in Jesus Christ give me authority to pray.
Divine Dialogue — Part Three

Exceptional Explanations
Reality is not a hoax. Scriptural knowledge will provide secure answers
Divine Dialogue — Part Four

Triple Torch
Discovering God's favor in a triplet's life
Divine Dialogue — Part Five

PASTORAL HEALTH CARE PART I

Discovering GOD'S *Sufficiency*

Going Beyond Ourselves and Experiencing the Supernatural

JOHN F. GILLETTE
Teaching Pastor, Pastor Health Care Minister
WITH JOY E. GILLETTE

Chapbook Press

Schuler Books
2660 28th Street SE
Grand Rapids MI 49512

www.schulerbooks.com/chapbook-press

Discovering God's Sufficiency: Going beyond ourselves and experiencing the supernatural

Copyright © 2016 — John F. Gillette. All rights reserved. Published 2016. Printed at Schuler Books, Chapbook Press, Grand Rapids, Michigan, in the United States of America.

Secon Edition 2020

Excerpts taken from Discovering God's Presence: A Pastoral Health Care Devotional, © 2015 by Dr. John F. Gillette, D.Min.

Distribution contact:at jjgillette@comcast.net.

ISBN 13: 9781943359530

Library of Congress Control Number: 2016959954

Cover photo: Greg Rakozy/Unsplash
Cover Design: Frank Gutbrod Graphic Design
Book typist: Michael Sharp

Printed in the United States of America

The Pastoral Health Care Discovery Series was produced to help during difficult trials in life. It was developed through five volumes.

Adjustments are shared through God's sufficiency. It provides a basic spiritual solution strategy. We have to affirm, accept and adjust to God's plan of action. His superiority, sovereignty and sufficiency will bring victory.

Empowerment is given through God's love. The receiving of his Son Jesus Christ provides power. Historical facts declare the truth.

Enablement is given through God's counsel. Instruction, illumination and application provides the growing process in grace.

Encouragement is given through the awareness of God's kingdom. Learning to accept God's perspective is necessary. The Holy Spirit will travel with us in the present and the future.

Contentment is given through God's heart. The meditation model is the method to follow.

It is with great affection that I dedicate this book series to my wife, Joy, who radiates God's grace. We wrote this Pastoral Health Care Series together.

Applying God's spiritual solutions to meet us in difficult trials has become even more practical in my life with the recent death of my dear wife, Joy. This book has been reproduced in her memory. While the content is the same, my dedication has become more personal than ever before. The separation is painful but as I gather my suffering and feelings of incompleteness, I will succeed with God's peace and presence. The guidelines of this book have brought blessing to our life together. We have pursued them with great persistence. I am assured that she is in God's presence, rejoicing and at peace. I will be with her to experience God's eternal presence someday as well.

". . . blessed are they who put their trust in Him."
Psalm 2:12

Table of Contents

Chapter 1
Death and Separation *01*

Chapter 2
Open Heart Surgery *08*

Chapter 3
God's Instruction *21*

Chapter 4
Confident Builder *50*

Chapter 5
Supernatural Power *71*

Chapter 6
The Promise of Peace *79*

Chapter 7
The Promise of Victory *85*

Chapter 8
The Promise of Hope *89*

Assignment: Encouraging Activities *100*

About the Author *103*

Death and Separation

My heart has been troubled. In August 2017, I lost my best friend and lover, my wife Joy. We were in a terrible accident. A lot can be said about the accident as it made the headline news on television, radio and social media. A car hit us while we were walking our dogs. Joy, my wife, was taken from me. I believe the Holy Spirit and the angels took her to the presence of Jesus Christ. I was hospitalized and spent many months in rehabilitation. Our family has experienced the terrible death and everything that follows. I have discovered the obtaining confidence in my troubled heart through believing God's Word. It is a long process but it will work. Read the Bible's solution slowly and put it into action. God will help us. He cares.

Affirm God's Essence and Compassions

I need to witness God's power and sovereignty in every day I live. I know He has the strength and love to produce it. It starts with me affirming His absolutes. Everything I do has its foundation on Him. The Bible says, "Ye believe in God," John 14:1; this is the starting point to go beyond ourselves and experience the supernatural. I am able to obtain confidence in my troubled heart through believing God's Word. It's not a mindless fluttering of the heart but a presentation of following God's words.

God is a Spirit. He is nonmaterial. He is invisible. He has the attributes of personhood. He displays emotions intellect and will. We see the reality of God in what He does not in what He looks like. God wants to be intimate with us. He says, "Believe also in me", John 14:1. Believing God provides confidence in the truth…"He is the way." Faith provides confidence and is a gift. It is a decision to respond to the Bible and practice it. We have to learn to trust Jesus Christ. Belief, trust and faith provide assurance during difficult times. Our spirit must be in touch with the Holy Spirit regardless of circumstances.

Accept God's Endearment and Knowledge

I am obtaining confidence in my troubled heart through believing God's Word. He said in John 14:2-3, "In my Father's house are many mansions…I will come back and take you to be with me that you also may be where I am". Calmness starts to take place when I realize heaven is a real place. Heaven is the place where God dwells and where Jesus sits today at the right hand of the Father. In 2 Peter 1:11 heaven is described as a "kingdom". In 1 John 1:4 it is an "inheritance." In Hebrews 11:16 it's described as "a city". And in Hebrews 11:16, it's described as "home". God wants us to call him "daddy" (Romans 8:15). The word Abba is the Aramaic equivalent of "daddy". It refers to endearment and respect. God is love and that love abides in us (I John 4:16). His home provides beauty and love. My intimacy with him will grow through fellowship with Him and my eternal home will be my destiny. He loves me, cares for me and knows what is best for me. This helps me to be confident in my troubled heart.

I am obtaining confidence in my troubled heart through believing God's Word. He said, "If you had known me, ye should have known my Father also." The word 'know' is used 141 times in John's Gospel, but it does not always carry the same meaning. Calmness starts when I have a deeper relationship with a person. He has the attributes of emotion, intellect and will. He has no beginnings. He is an eternal being. He is self-generating. He is changeless in His person. He is changeless in His character. He is able to restore my soul (Psalm 23:2-3). He is sufficient to provide confidence in my troubled heart.

I am obtaining confidence in my troubled heart through believing God's Word. He said, "If ye shall ask any thing in my name, I will do it" (John 14:14). Calmness will take place as I pray in faith (John 14:12). This is a promise to claim. Praying in faith is a decision to accept His word and glorify His name. What He says to do, do it, and expect with hope. "For it is God which worketh in you", Philippians 2:13. Faith releases the power of God in our lives. We have to learn to ask what Jesus would ask, what would please Him? Through obedience in Him, motivated by love I will obtain confidence.

Obtaining confidence is provided through the four thoughts that you have just read. Each day think about one and claim it for yourself. It is promised. The next three will become a result of obtaining confidence.

Adjust to God's Indwelling Peace

I am obtaining confidence in my troubled heart through believing God's Word. He said, "I will pray the Father and he shall give you another comforter, he may abide with you forever." John 14:16 Calmness is assured. The Holy Spirit, our "Comforter" is called alongside to assist. He strengthens us to full life. He is our encourager and advocate. The Spirit of truth uses the word of truth to guide us into the will and the work of

God. There is no need to have a troubled heart. God dwelling within me makes the difference.

I am obtaining confidence in my troubled heart through believing God's Word. He said, "He that hath my commandments, and keepeth them, it is he that loveth me. He that loveth me shall be loved of my Father and I will love him and will manifest myself to Him," John 14:21.

Calmness for my spirit, soul and body will be present through His manifestation of himself. If we love God and obey Him, He will manifest His love to us in a deeper way each day. We have to yield to the spirit of truth and permit Him to teach us and guide us. Little faith will move us toward heaven but great faith will bring heaven to our souls.

I am obtaining confidence in my troubled heart through believing God's Word. He said, "Peace I leave with you, my peace I give unto you not as the world giveth, give I unto you. Let not your heart be troubled, neither let it be afraid." John 14:27

I have been walking by sight and depend on the externals. His word gives us His peace (John 14:27), His love (John 15:9-10) and His joy (John 15:11). We have the Savior above us, we have the spirit within us and the word before us. Jesus is the master of the situation and He enables us to take control of our lives as we surrender to Him. I am following this scripture day by day. I am learning to rely on these assurances. They are produced within the heart of God's sufficiency.

Open Heart Surgery

The Bible says, "He made us and we are his."[1] This is a favorite Psalm of many followers of Jesus. It is a great doxology that is found in Psalm 100. I have used the first verse many times to introduce my concerts. "Make a joyful noise unto the Lord."[2] I thought at least I'm biblical if the instrumentalist sound like noise rather than music. We could divide the Psalm into five sermons. Shout with praises to the Lord is found in verse one. Serve the Lord with gladness is in verse two. My primary text is in verse three. It says, 'know that he is Lord.' Enter into his gates is found in the fourth verse. The chapter ends with receive his mercy.

---

1   Psalm 100:3
2   Psalm 100:1

During times of hardship, suffering, trials and the unknown, we can find rest. During my preparation for open heart surgery, the doctor said to think about something good and this scripture came to my memory. It has continued to bring his power, presence and peace to my soul. It will do the same for you.

Can anyone fix our troubles? The answer is yes. We don't suffer apart from the knowledge of God. Do not be intimidated by all the talk. God knows all the details. Keep in mind God's character rather than his creation. He has the big picture in view. This is not a formula, remedy, prescription or cure. It is the course I have followed to conquer. Every day I have to affirm, accept and adjust to God's plan of action.

As far as I am concerned, the Bible is absolute in truth. In my deepest worry and concern, I have discovered the spiritual solution strategy works for me. I have been trained to look to the Holy Scriptures for answers. They have proved themselves as a profitable resource. I have found peace and rest when I did not think I would be able to. Just think of it… "people who know their God will display strength and take action."[3] Let us study the text and experience strength, support and steadfastness.

We have to affirm God's intervention. In times of difficulties, it is hard to read, study or do research to find an answer. We may only be able to pray. This is the best reaction. I had to affirm that 'He' in the text refers to God. Pray the "Lord's Prayer"[4] and put your own communication with it.

Our Father refers to our creator God. He is personal, intimate, self-existent, self-sufficient and eternal. Things do not just happen. He can do whatever he wants because it is all his.[5] There is no chance happening, no luck and no mistakes. Both good and bad fall under his control. He has absolute rule over the affairs of men. He is sovereign. He works all things after the counsel of his own will.[6] We have a relationship with him

---

[3] Daniel 11:32
[4] Matthew 6:9-13
[5] Psalm 24:1
[6] Ephesians 1:11

through faith in his son.[7] Forsaking all I trust him.[8] I know he has my best interest in mind.

'Who art in heaven' — God is spirit. He exists everywhere at the same time. He is in us. We live, move and exist in him. We can be assured in our total dependence upon him because he is present. His kingdom provides spiritual guidance through mercy, truth, righteousness, peace and harmony. Our citizenship is on the earth and in heaven. Our attitude on earth should be directed from heaven. God's residence is everywhere. Let's obtain our instruction from him and 'seek his kingdom.'[9]

'Hallowed be thy name' is the central attribute of God. All others stem from it. Respect, reverence, awe, appreciation, honor, glory, adoration and worship are included in this word. It is the doxology of the prayer. "Great is the Lord and greatly to be praised"[10] This part of the prayer provides the empowerment to accomplish that which follows.

---

7   Romans 10:9, 10
8   A child's definition
9   Matthew 6:33
10 Psalm 57:11

'*Thy name, kingdom and will be done on earth as it is in heaven*' refers to his rules for us to follow. We need to be conscious of his presence. He has the plan for our lives. We have to learn to pray in his name which means we place his name on each request. We have to learn to allow him to reign in our lives. We have to replace our will for his will.

'*Give us, forgive us and lead us*' includes three kinds of prayers. We can bring our daily needs to him. He can provide for our well-being. He can take care of our emotional, physical, spiritual and directional concerns.[11] He wants us to be intimate with him. Confession of sin and adoration given to him will start the path to close fellowship. The third kind of prayer is intercession. This is when we forget ourselves and bring others to the attention of God. God wants to hear our requests.

'*For thine is the kingdom and power and the glory forever.*' This is the benediction in the prayer. We serve under his kingdom. We live

---
11   Psalm 23

with his strength. All our needs are met through him. In our struggles, we have to affirm who 'He' is. It will give us victory. He who dwells in the secret place of the most high shall abide under the shadow of the Almighty. He is our refuge and fortress, in him we can trust.[12] The first step for endurance and overcoming is affirmation. His intervention will be felt.

We have to accept God's indwelling. In times of discomfort, discouragement, discontent, distress, depression and dread, we can be assured that he is working on our behalf. The Scripture teaches that God the Father,[13] God the Son[14] and God the Spirit,[15] are within us. Christians have possession of the divine nature. The individual persons of the godhead lives and works through us.[16] Our negatives are part of his positive program. God knows where he wants to take us and how he wants to get us there. God is near

---
12 Psalm 91:1, 2
13 Ephesians 4:6
14 Colossians 1:27
15 1 Corinthians 6:19
16 Romans 8:9

when we feel him and when we do not feel him. He counsels with his promises that he is going to accomplish something if we think so or not.

We have to accept that the 'us' in the text refers to our redeemer God that has become our substitute. He says, "Come unto me."[17] These are life changing words, but they cannot be heard by our sinful, rebellious and stubborn minds without a sovereignly bestowed spiritual awakening. The divine initiative is in verse 27 and a free offer to all in verses 28-30.[18] These are the steps to follow to trust Jesus. "All ye that labor and are heavy laden" are words that describe our condition. We have to recognize our sinful condition. The first element in trusting Jesus is total dependency. "And I will give you rest," — liberation is given through Jesus. We can entrust our spirit, soul and body to him because of who he is and what he has done. He is the pre-existing Son of God who became man in order to reveal the Father and bring eternal life through his death and resurrection.[19]

---

17 Matthew 11:28-30
18 Discovering God's Favor, JFG, p. 13
19 John 20:30, 31

"Take my yoke upon you and learn of me, for I am meek and lowly in heart." A complete turnaround is necessary. Through Jesus, we can turn from sin and replace it with faith. This is not an intellectual exercise but a whole heart change.

"For my yoke is easy and my burden is light." The yoke is a symbol of submission and it is joyful. Salvation occurs when God changes the heart and unbelievers turn from sin to Christ.[20] Faith is the process for Jesus to enter the heart and dwell there.[21] Genuine conversion involves five essential elements. We cannot interpret spiritual reality with human reason. We have to accept God's invitation as a child with a sense of dependency. The authority comes through the revelation of God. Man-made religion is fruitless and vain. Only by God's revelation from his son are we able to receive divine truth.

We cannot earn our salvation. Finding truth comes through Jesus which involves a complete turnaround. Faith is the flip side of repentance.

---
20 Colossians 1:13
21 Ephesians 3:17

We turn from sin to the Savior. It is a turning of the whole heart to Christ. Submission is found in the word 'yoke' and discipleship is in the words "and learn of me." Together they imply obedience.[22] The second step for endurance and overcoming is acceptance. His indwelling will be felt.

We have to make some adjustments through God's illumination when we suffer, become helpless, fear the unknown and are hopeless, decide to face life realistically and with absolutes. We know life is not a bed of roses. The spiritual solution strategy does work. After we affirm God's presence and accept his supernatural power through his son, we can learn to demonstrate the fruit of the spirit. Renewing our thinking process will take place. We can be successful with a continual filling of the Holy Spirit.[23] Remember, we are new creations in Jesus Christ.[24]

Love is the highest of virtues. It has to be our priority. We can make the right decisions

---

22 The Gospel according to Jesus, John F. Mac Arthur, Jr. p. 115
23 Ephesians 5:18
24 1 Corinthians 5:17

because God is in us. Meeting his conditions is necessary.[25] Loving with intensity will deepen our fellowship. It will produce a selfless, serving, sympathetic and secure heart. We can follow the example of the gospel writers. Matthew was a tax collector for Rome. He was despised and belonged with the outcast in the community. He was good at keeping records. He knew his Old Testament. He preached love through a changed life. He answered Jesus' call to follow. The feast he gave at his home was the means to share Jesus with others. His life after meeting Jesus became selfless. He looked at life from God's perspective rather than his own. Mark was brought up in a home of prayer. He was tutored by Peter, Paul and Barnabas. He demonstrated love through service.

Luke was well trained and believed to be a physician. He was a companion of Paul. He examined all the authentic records and consulted every available eyewitness. He speaks of the

---

25 Matthew 6:33

humanity of Jesus and shared his love through having a sympathetic heart.

John speaks of the divinity of Christ. He gives a theological rather than a biographical or historical presentation of the person of Christ. He was with Jesus constantly. What he experienced under the teaching of Jesus Christ proved that he was God incarnate. He demonstrated love through having a secure heart.

Love will produce joy in spite of suffering and adverse circumstances. Various trials will come but our sovereign God is in charge. He knows what we can bear.[26] We have to choose to receive joy through obedience and faith. Joy is a divine happiness that undergirds all emotional reactions. It is a life of enthusiasm and beauty. A relationship with Jesus Christ, a growing fellowship with a sovereign God and worship with the Holy Spirit will lead the way. God is working in us. We have to yield our agenda for the day to him. He is the boss. We have to make decisions in his will. Joy will be the end result. The

---

26 1 Corinthians 10-13

adjustments are hard to accomplish because the flesh is weak. The peace of God will become reality. We have to accept the authority of Jesus.[27] Believing the supernatural is not through the natural, it is developing through the supernatural. God has fully expressed himself in Christ.[28] We cannot be careless in our effort to follow Jesus. We must have a deliberate desire. The third step for endurance and overcoming is making the adjustments. His illumination will be felt.

The Bible says, "He made us and we are his."[29] God the Father has chosen us, God the Son has purchased us and God the Holy Spirit has sealed us. "According as he hath chosen us,"[30] this means to pick out for one's self.[31] The word 'elect' in 1 Peter 1:2 is the noun form of the verb 'chosen.' God knows everything by virtue of who he is. God's knowledge and eternal purpose intersects with human choice in such a way that we have real

---

27 Hebrews 1:1, 2
28 John 3:16
29 Psalm 100:3
30 Ephesians 1:4
31 Wuest's word study, p. 30

choices to make and yet those choices fulfill God's purposes to accomplish his goal. God does make provisions for all but he has elected some, leaving us with a choice but guarantees his plans.[32] "To whom we have redemption through his blood, the forgiveness of sins, according to the riches of his grace,"[33] we have been released from sin. The word 'sin' means to step aside. Grace is God's awesome favor. His grace provides the power to overcome our difficulties. He gives wisdom and understanding. We have been sealed with the Holy Spirit of promise.[34] The seal is the Holy Spirit. It is a finished transaction. We have his permanent residence. We are eternally secure. The pure grace of God brings about the fruitfulness. Our creator God has chosen us, our redeemer God has purchased us and our comforter God has sealed us. We are 'His Very Own.'[35]

---

32 Awesome God, Tony Evans, p. 145
33 Hebrews 1:7, 8
34 Ephesians 1:13
35 Our theme song

God's Instruction

To change feelings, we must change thinking. Inaction will bring misery.[36] Learn to apply the Scripture to your life. The result will bring strength, support and steadfastness.

Learning to live every moment in God's presence requires applying his instruction. Out of all the promises I have learned, this one seems to cover all of them. As I draw near to him, he gives me the instruction I need to follow. He equips me to face whatever is before me. This provides the enablement and mindset needed to live a full and complete life (John 10:10). As he draws near to me, I am able to sense his presence. This provides confidence and joy in knowing that he has my best interest in mind even if I don't understand at the time.

---

36 Christian Counseling, Gary R. Collins, p. 93

I am going to share what I am practicing in order to overcome weakness, temptations, health issues, decision making and just plain troublesome issues. Someone said, "thinking right always precedes acting right." I would add spiritual insight and application will cause us to think right and act right. I have discovered that the promises work. Put into action Jesus' words and you will find contentment and rest.

"Draw near to me and I will draw near to you" is found in James 4:8. James, the brother of Jesus, was used through the Holy Spirit to pen these words. James was ministering in Jerusalem. The church was persecuted and driven out of the city and scattered. He says do not be alarmed or sad. The child of God may rejoice victoriously even in the darkest hour. To rejoice I have to not only obtain knowledge (the facts) but it involves experiential knowledge (doing). Most of all, it involves an illumined heart (Holy Spirit counsel). I am excited to know that when I do not get it (the answer for difficult issues), I can always ask for wisdom (1:5). I can find the purpose in the predicament. I am not going to doubt God. He has given me faith and I trust the faith giver. God is all he claims to be.

I have to learn to listen to his Word and then do it. I have to learn to be submissive and live life with spiritual discernment. I have to learn to practice self-control. God's grace is at work. Practicing submission to God and resisting the enemy will pave the way for me to draw near to God and assure me of him drawing near to me.

Drawing near to God involves an attitude of helplessness which will result in enablement. In Jesus' own words, he says "Blessed are the poor in spirit for theirs is the Kingdom of heaven." (Matthew 5:3). He also says in his model prayer "Hallowed be thy name"(Matthew 6:9). He gives the instruction on how to draw near and he gives the source of power behind it. I have to come to the realization that dependence upon God is necessary. I have to acknowledge sin in my life. I have to receive and believe in Jesus Christ (Acts 16:31; Romans 10:9-10). His enablement takes place when a relationship develops with him and I learn what "thy will be done on earth as it is in heaven" means on a daily basis. I have become a member of the Kingdom of heaven. I have a double citizenship on earth and heaven. My life is nothing less than "Christ in you, the hope of glory" (Colossians 1:27). Natural life has a beginning but no end. My eternal life will provide fellowship with God for all eternity. My life on earth is preparation for heaven and drawing closer to him.

Helplessness refers to not being able to help oneself. To be "poor in spirit" means that I have emptied myself of me – now there is room to be filled. The world promotes self-sufficiency or at the present time (2010) government sufficiency, yet God dwells with the man whose heart is broken (Isaiah 57:15). When this decision is made, the promise of inheriting the Kingdom will provide enablement. Power, energy and strength are found in the centerpiece of God's attributes "Hallowed be thy name" (Matthew 6:9). This opens up a whole dimension of reverence, respect, awe, appreciation, honor, glory, adoration and worship. To hallow God's name means to hold his matchless being in reverence so that we will believe what he says and will obey him. When I live by faith and bear fruit in my character, I will exalt God's name. God has asked me to live in harmony with who he is and has stated this in his Word. I must understand my helplessness and promised enablement. When I fear God, I will have the necessary ingredient of life which opens the door to everything good (Psalm 111:10; Proverbs 1:7,8,13).

I know through personal experience God's enablement through helplessness. I can talk about sickness (heart disease, cancer) and about several friends with a variety of physical or mental illnesses. I can share about financial stress and looking for a job without success. I can include inferiority complex and the lack of confidence – the list is long.

Enablement comes through understanding the Biblical phrase "It is he that hath made us and we are his" (Psalm 100:3). I have seen this positive phrase bring spiritual enablement for many besides myself. We can be assured in our total dependence upon him that it will provide authority because he is all-powerful. I cannot Lord, but you can. Abiding in Jesus is the secret of enablement.

Drawing near to God involves an attitude of repentance which will result in comfort. In Jesus' own words he says, "Blessed are they that mourn for they shall be comforted" (Matthew 5:4). He also says in his model prayer "Thy kingdom come," heavenly comfort will come to us (Matthew 6:10). He gives the instruction on how to draw near, and he gives the source of power behind it.

I have come to the realization that repentance is necessary if I am going to draw near to him. I have asked myself often, "do I ever mourn for sin that has been allowed in my life; do I experience anguish over lost souls, and the disobedience of followers of Jesus?" I know that I can experience God's compassion through my repentance and be renewed.

Mourning refers to a sincere sorrow for sin. God hates sin. I should also. It grieves him but I like to make excuses for it. Tolerance, deception and blindness – add your own favorite word to the list that creates a blockage to growth. Repentance means a change of mind. It is a thorough change in the heart from sin to God. It is a gift of God (Acts 5:31; 11:18; Romans 2:4). I have to be mournful not only because of the consequences of sin and the baseness of sin but also the divine compassion provided in salvation.

Repentance will challenge me to put the Scripture into action…"put to death – whatever belongs to your earthly nature…" (Colossians 3:5). Sometimes I forget my responsibility. I have to make a personal decision to pursue holiness. I have to learn to put to death the misdeeds of my body. I have to destroy the strength and vitality of sin as it tries to reign in my body. Just think of it – my body is the temple of the Holy Spirit. He will do it. He is sufficient for this work. Conviction will start the path toward a holy life.

Keep in mind "without holiness no one will see the Lord" (Hebrews 12:14). I want to be drawn near to God.

The world's values that are everywhere present must be replaced with God's. I have to let God remake me and not allow the world to squeeze me in (Romans 12:2). I have learned that only through God's Word can my mind be renewed. It takes conviction and obedience to pave the way to fulfill God's desires for me (John 14:21). The Scripture must be strongly fixed in my mind and heart. It will become the dominant influence on my thoughts, attitudes and actions. I like memorizing Scripture because I know it works (Psalm 119:11). I believe conviction and obedience linked together with confession will bring comfort in my repentance. Confession is necessary every day.

God hates sin and I must be sensitive to it. I must confess it and accept God's comfort in my repentance. I must let his Word work in my life. I must hide his Word in my heart. I have used the word "must" several times. It is important to do what I am trying to emphasize or I will fail. To understand what is right or wrong to do, I have to ask myself, "is it helpful physically, spiritually and mentally? Does it bring me under its power? Does it hurt others? Does it glorify God?" (I Corinthians 6:12; 8:13; 10:31).

Drawing near to God involves an attitude of surrender which will result in a controlled life. In Jesus' own words he said, "Blessed are the meek for they shall inherit the earth" (Matthew 5). He also said in his model prayer "Thy will be done on earth as it is in heaven" this meekness is characterized in heaven (Matthew 6:10). He gives the instruction and how to draw near, and he gives the source of power behind it. I have come to the realization that meekness in my life will bring about a controlled life. Meekness refers to living for the glory of God. There is no room for self-will. It is not thinking of asserting my own rights. Meekness is not weakness but a display of strength. Meekness is brought into my life through God's grace. I have to learn to accept God's dealings with me without resistance or dispute. No more rebelling or fighting against God. It flows from the heart of humility and submission.

I believe that when I have the three 'thys" in the right perspective in my life (found in Jesus' model prayer), I will experience the meekness characteristic. I am glad that the Holy Spirit makes this possible (Romans 8:26,27). I have to practice faith and the certainty of the Holy Spirit's indwelling. I have to surrender my will to his will. I have to place Jesus' name on everything. The word 'thy' emphasizes God's rule. His sovereignty is in charge. He has absolute control over all of creation. I have to live life in relationship with his sovereignty. I don't have to figure out the plan.

The sovereign kingdom rule has to be followed. Meekness and control are the fruit of obedience. I have to learn to switch on the confidence button by turning to God and away from sin, switch on the confidence button by allowing my inner judge of moral issues to be in tune with Jesus Christ, switch on the confidence button by making decisions through a righteous common sense and switch on the confidence button by obeying the special assignments given to me. "The Kingdom of God is not meat and drink but righteousness, peace and joy in the Holy Ghost" (Romans 14:17).

Drawing near to God involves an attitude of craving which will result in satisfaction. In Jesus' own words he says, "Blessed are they that hunger and thirst after righteousness for they shall be filled" (5:4). He also says in his model prayer "Give us this day our daily bread" (Matthew 6:10). He gives the instruction on how to draw near and he gives the source of power behind it. I have to come to the realization that craving after righteousness is absolutely necessary. Only when this takes place will I find contentment.

When I have a craving for something, I cannot leave it alone. It has a driving force behind it. It pushes me forward. This can be a good thing that takes place yet also bad. I am looking at the positive side and not the negative. Proof of my spiritual rebirth is found in my desire to pursue after righteousness with hunger and thirst. The inner passion is a blessing. Being poor/helpless, being mournful/repentant and being meek/surrendered will cause a deep earnest desire to search the Scriptures. This will bring satisfaction, fulfillment and contentment. Practicing having an appetite for good food is a good thing. What I eat will reveal the man I really am.

Craving after righteousness will take place as I study his Word. A few weeks ago I was looking at some of my previous sermons. They are bound into a dozen or so books. I found one based upon Psalm 119:33-40 – "quicken thou me—quicken me in thy righteousness." The word 'quicken' means in Hebrew to make alive, to refresh and in English it refers to a thought of adventure and becoming active. I discovered through activating the thoughts in verses 33-40 that they will produce a craving heart for righteousness. "Teach me" (v.33) indicates that a foundation has been laid. The master teacher has brought the lesson to my ears and has established my way. The teaching has made me alive. "Give me understanding" (v. 34) has brought discernment and correct insight. It is not only information and knowledge but a diligence to pursue it. Understanding has made me alive. "I shall observe" (v. 34); careful watching and exercising great care has made me alive. "I delight in the path" (v. 35), receiving the instruction, understanding the Word and careful observation has brought pleasure. A deep affection has been cultivated and has made me alive. "Incline my heart" (v. 36); through God's testimonies, my being has been made alive. With the right purpose in mind, the attitude is to covet Jesus Christ. "Turn away" (v. 37) allows my eyes to feast upon Jesus and not my own vanity. Help me to move in the right direction and be made alive. "Establish thy Word" (v. 38); my heart has been made alive through the respect and reverence that has integrated into my soul for Jesus.

"Turn away my reproach" (v. 39); I have learned that your Word is sound, beneficial, righteous, fruitful and pleasant. I have been made alive because your judgments are good. "Behold, I have longed after thy precepts" (v. 40); Craving for righteousness will be produced through an intense, sensitive and energetic response to God's Word. I have to realize the source of quickening is through the infusion of the Holy Spirit. I have to realize that I have to respond to his quickening. I have to make a decision to feed upon the Scripture. I am not a victim of worldliness or my own weaknesses. "Quicken thou me in thy way." This is possible because of Jesus' model prayer. He said "Give us this day our daily bread" (Matthew 6"11). This refers to all of my physical needs. When I am dependent upon him, he provides all my needs. Boldness in the Holy Spirit and confidence will empower me. I am thankful for the fact that he provides food, clothes, shelter and especially his presence in health or sickness. I have discovered this in his Word that has power to quicken me. Drawing near to God involves an attitude of empathy which will result in mercy. In Jesus' own words he says, "Blessed are the merciful for they shall obtain mercy" (Matthew 5:7). He also says in his model prayer "Forgive us our debts as we forgive our debtors" (Matthew 6:12). He gives the instruction on how to draw near and he gives the source of power behind it. I have come to the realization that experiencing empathy will bring mercy.

Mercy is defined as being compassionate. Compassion is having a feeling of deep sympathy. Sympathy is the ability to share the feelings of another. This leads to empathy. Empathy is identifying with an experience of the feeling and thoughts of another. Someone told me that it is like getting in the skin of another. Mercy becomes a part of my life because I have obtained mercy. The Holy Spirit produces mercy. Jesus himself became the ultimate example of this when he cried from the cross, "Father, forgive them for they know not what they do" (Luke 23:34).

When I get in touch with God, I can feel his mercy at work on my behalf. It started when

I trusted in him (Ephesians 2:4-7) and he gave me a clean heart (Acts 15:9) and peace within (Romans 5:1). When I receive mercy, I then can share his mercy with others. I pray that I can be sensitive to others that cross my path. I hope I can sense their hopelessness and need. I desire to come alongside of them.

Drawing near to God involves an attitude of authenticity which will result in seeing God. In Jesus' own words he says "Blessed are the pure in heart for they shall see God" (Matthew 5:8). He also says in his model prayer "And lead us not into temptation but deliver us" (Matthew 6:13). He gives the instruction and he gives the source of power behind it. I have come to the realization that purity will cause my heart to see God.

God is doing a work in me. He is conforming me into the image of Christ (Romans 8:29) whose image consists in "righteousness and true holiness." (Ephesians 4:24). Purity of heart is a part of my election and redemption (Ephesians 1:4; Titus 2:14).

This is not sinlessness (I John 1:8) but the truth within (Psalm 51:6). It means a single heart. I am not divided between God and the world. I realize that this calls for radical living. The world praises pride not humility. The world endorses sin. The world is at war with God. Righteousness will cause persecution. Conflict will take place. Since my life has been transformed by the grace of God, I will see him. Daily faith will bring me into his presence. I might be called peculiar (Titus 2:14) but I have been chosen by the Father, purchased by the Son and sealed by the Spirit. I will see God.

Drawing near to God involves an attitude of harmony which will result in being called children of God. In Jesus' own words he said, "Blessed are the peacemakers for they will be called children of God" (Matthew 5:9). He also said in his model prayer "For thine is the Kingdom" (Matthew 6:13). He gives the instruction and how to draw near and he gives the source of power behind it. I have come to the realization that harmony with God will bring peace. With the regeneration power of the gospel in my life, I have experienced peace with God. I am able to be an ambassador of God's message of peace to a troubled world because I daily experience the peace of God in my life. My ministry is to be a channel of God's mercy, purity and peace.

There have been many times that I have stood between enemies. The Holy Spirit apparently was present to protect me. My attitude of peace caused such a stir and confusion that those enemies didn't know what to do. They would lay down their fists and with humility say "what should we do?" That gave me the opportunity to share the true peacemaker.

Drawing near to God involves an attitude of victory during persecution because it will bring about the Kingdom of heaven. "Blessed are they which are persecuted for righteousness sake" (Matthew 5:10). He also said in his model prayer "For thine is the power and the glory forever" (Matthew 6:13). He gives the instruction and how to draw near and he gives the source of power behind it. I have come to the realization that if persecuted, I am assured of the Kingdom of heaven. The Bible says, "Yea and all that will live godly in Christ Jesus shall suffer persecution" (2 Timothy 3:12). I know that suffering can be experienced through being kept from ones goal. I know that suffering can be experienced through being tempted through social enterprise. I know suffering can be felt through the presence of the world. I know suffering can be produced by fellow Christians. Some day I may experience suffering through physical abuse.

I can experience his power, presence and peace (Psalm 16:8). The key to spiritual victory is to stay close to God. I have to learn to practice God's presence all day long. "The Lord is near to all who call on him" (Psalm 145:18). The songwriter has written "Have thine own way Lord." During persecution and peace, I am going to celebrate life in magnifying Jesus' name.

Jesus never promised ease to those of us he called to follow him. Reliance upon Jesus will cause radical living. Ridicule will most likely pursue us but keep in mind a reward will follow. Jesus lived through persecution, he died through persecution and he rose again after the persecution.

Drawing near to God will fulfill God's promise that he will draw near to me. When I apply Jesus' instruction and experience his power through his model prayer, the Holy Spirit will produce his fruit in my life. The word "blessed" (Matthew 5:1-12) truthfully becomes a description of my life.

I have come to the end of this study and yet I have to return to the beginning with the word "blessed." Blessed means happy. My inner being is happy because of the work of God in my life. The characteristics I have been sharing have been a result of believing.

- I am learning to be helpless (poor in spirit).
- I am learning to be repentive (mournful).
- I am learning to be surrendered (meek).
- I am learning to crave (hunger).

- I am learning to practice empathy (mercy).
- I am learning to be authentic (pure).
- I am learning to be in harmony (peacemaker).
- I am learning to be victorious in suffering (persecution).

I am blessed with the Holy Spirit's enablement to experience a "touch of heaven" here on earth through practicing these attributes. I am realizing God's rule and providence in my life on earth. I am looking forward to when the last enemy (sin and death) (I Corinthians 15:24-28) will be destroyed at the Lord's return.

I am drawing near to him every day as I practice the Lord's instructions. The day will come when he will draw near to me even with greater intensity. "Face to face, I will behold him, far beyond the starry sky, Face to face, in all his glory, I shall see him by and by!" The only condition is faith in God's Son, the Lord Jesus Christ. He said, "For God so loved the world that he gave his only begotten son, that whoever believes on him should not perish but have everlasting life" (John 3:16).

I love my home here on earth. A day does not go by that as I walk in the yard with my dogs that I don't forget to thank God for the beauty and pleasantness of the place he has given me to live. I realize that my happiness is wherever my family is, that's home. As I draw near to God and he draws near to me, I can call heaven my eternal home. Death does not end all. My spirit lives on and enters immediately into the very presence of God.

Death involves physical and spiritual separation. Physical death occurs when my spirit is separated from the body. Spiritual death is the eternal separation of the spirit from God. This means that as a believer, I will never be separated from God. Jesus said "He who hears my word and believes in him who sent me has everlasting life" (John 5:24). In the deepest sense of the word, I will never die. Jesus gave the promise, "whoever lives and believes in me shall never die" (John 11:25, 26). Jesus is my source of life. He is the resurrection and the life. My life between death and resurrection will be a time of joy, blessing and fellowship with Jesus. Drawing near to him starts a deep and sweet relationship that will continue into a greater depth in heaven.

I am learning to live my life with a double citizenship. I am glad that I am a citizen of the United States of America and also of the heavenly city. A day is coming when our present solar system will be burned with fire and will be replaced by a new heaven and a new earth (2 Peter 3:10). It will burst into flames with such intense heat that even the elements that make up matter will be dissolved. The sun, the moon, the planets and the distant stars will all be engulfed in flames but this will not be a tragedy. The Bible says that out of the ruins will emerge a glorious new world – my eternal home (Revelation 21:1,2).

As I draw near to God and he draws near to me, he will bring me into a wonderful life. In my eternal home which is a perfect society, I will realize my full spiritual potential as an individual. I will enter in an eternal fellowship with God. An endless variety of meaningful activities will take place. All imperfections of this life will be gone and positive blessings will be in abundance. My present knowledge of God, while real and precious, is incomplete. In heaven I will know him perfectly. I will behold the glory of his presence and faith will turn to sight (Revelation 21:3).

If my attitude is based upon submission and obedience, God will draw near to me. He says, "I will draw near to you." This gives me a sense of his presence and love. To understand God's love, I have to know God's eternal passion to accomplish his will in such a way that he is glorified. God's love is eternal. God was love before he created man or anything else. I have to learn to let God be God. His will and glory go hand in hand to produce his love. I am under his umbrella of love. He unfolds his will to achieve his glory in my life through love.

The ultimate definition of God's love is expressed in these words: action, sacrifice, beneficial, unconditional and emotional. I must learn to take every circumstance of life and glorify him. The challenge is to be consumed with his love. I must keep his purpose in mind and then inner strength will flow.

He says, "I will draw near to you." This gives me a sense of his presence and grace. I do not deserve grace but God has given it to me. It is his unmerited favor. Grace is designed to save me and keep me. The Scripture says, "Grow in the grace and knowledge of our Lord and Savior Jesus Christ." (2 Peter 3:18). God is sufficient. God's grace is his empowerment to overcome. It raises me above the problem and gives me power at the exact point when I want to quit. Grace instructs me in how to live. Grace gives victory where I didn't have it. Grace will give the ability to keep going. Grace is the exchanging of my life for Christ-like living in me. (Galatians 2:20). Grace is inner spiritual power and not outward religious conformity. I have been set free to enjoy Christ's life in me (Galatians 5:1). I am challenged to measure my growth in grace; if I am lacking, I ask for his grace (Galatians 5:22,23).

He says, "I will draw near to you." This gives me a sense of his presence and sovereignty. He has absolute rule and control over all of creation. This means he causes or allows everything. I have to put everything in life under that perspective. It certainly makes me think, act and live different. He has created everything and he owns everything. He can do as he pleases. (Psalm 115:3; 135:6). Everything that occurs does so under the hand of a sovereign God. No chance happenings, no luck, no mistakes. Good and bad fall under his control. God knows where he is going and allows me to make choices. He will achieve his intended purpose. His purpose is to receive glory. I exist to please him (I Corinthians 8:6). I obtain strength through him (Philippians 4:13). I have confidence in him (2 Timothy 1:12).

He says, "I will draw near to you." This gives me a sense of his presence and glory. God's inner core is a radiating light (I Timothy 6:15,16). God's visible glory was most fully seen in the person of Jesus Christ (John 1:1,14,18). Jesus Christ is God in the flesh (Matthew 17:1-8). I am to tell of his glory (Psalm 96:1-3). His glory will put a glow in my life. Transformation is a growing adventure. I have to learn to submit to God's glory (I Corinthians 10:31). I glorify him when I

- Show Christ like character (John 15:8)
- Apply Biblical truths (Matthew 5:16)
- Practice sexual purity (I Corinthians 6:18-20)
- Daily confess sins (Joshua 7:19)
- Live by faith (Romans 4:19-21)
- Proclaim his Word (2 Thessalonians 3:1)
- Do his will (John 17:41)
- Confess his Son (Philippians 2:10)

He says, "I will draw near to you." This gives me a sense of his presence and justice. God is good, kind, loving and forgiving. He is also just and I must take his wrath seriously. God must judge sin because of the justice of his law and the righteousness of his character. He takes no pleasure in punishing the unrighteous (Ezekiel 33:11). He will judge all men according to their deeds (I Peter 1:17). The word "wrath" indicates God's intense displeasure of sin. God's wrath is not cruel but just. There are two sides to God's response to sin. "Thou hast loved righteousness and hated wickedness" (Psalm 45:7). I am glad that God is patient (2 Peter 3:9). My only way of escape is through God's substitute, Jesus who "delivers me from the wrath to come" (I Thessalonians 1:10). Christ died for me (Romans 5:8,9).

He says, "I will draw near to you." This gives me a sense of his presence and wisdom. Wisdom is knowing that God's purpose is to glorify himself. Wisdom moves all events, all people and all circumstances toward his purpose. Whether I resist or cooperate, he is still going to achieve his purpose. Wisdom is the ability to use my spiritual character, Biblical knowledge, common sense and circumstances and blending them together. I have an infinitely wise God that tells me to ask him for wisdom. I am not where I am by luck or chance. The infinitely wise God has been ordering my life. I was in his mind before the creation of the earth. He will give wisdom to make the response that will bring him glory. A determined will to agree with "thy will be done" is the answer. Ask in faith and anticipate the answer. Mixing human wisdom and divine wisdom doesn't work (James 3:16-18). To obtain wisdom, I have to admit that I need it. I have to stand in awe of God (Psalm 111:10). I have to study the Word. I need to pray for wisdom (James 1:5).

I will draw near to God. I have accepted the challenge and have followed his instruction through his "blessed sayings" and his model prayer with intensity. The fruit has become the test results. This has been evident in my life with his presence of love, grace, sovereignty, glory, justice and wisdom. He will keep to his Word. Experience it yourself! Why not try it! God's presence involves applying his instruction.

Confident Builder

I have been able to follow God's plan of action in my life through practicing his promises. This scripture, Psalm 100:3, has proven to be profitable. Read the examples given to bring comfort. Affirm his intervention that provides peace. Accept his indwelling and experience victory. Adjust to God's illumination with hope.

Learning to live every moment in God's presence requires claiming his promises. In my book "Discovering God's Favor," I have shared God's faithfulness through using Psalm 23 as a foundation for my childhood events that needed a touch from a faithful God. Take time to read it because it will enhance your spiritual growth. I have great benefits in having a relationship with God the Father through his son, Jesus Christ and the guidance of the Holy Spirit. The divine genius is working daily on my behalf.

I am interested in accepting God's provision for unknown issues that come up in my life. I want to share how this Psalm-poem (Psalm 23) has secured the path for me. It starts with authority that can transform the seeking heart. Deity is suddenly facing me. I can handle anything with God alongside of me. All his attributes go into action. In my book, I write about his attributes and later I share thoughts about his name. They have become confidence builders. There is no losing of ground when I know in whom I believe. I have a growing intimate relationship. "The Lord is my Shepherd." It is hard to comprehend or believe but I have communication with God my creator-sustainer-redeemer and Lord.

There is no deficiency in my life. He provides the promise, "I shall not be in want." Contentment can settle me. Only he can provide such rest and peace. He is in charge and the controller of all things. The unknown is directed by his hand of mercy. This is only the beginning. I am able to shout and jump with joy because an infinite, holy, self-existent God in whom I have found has provided the way.

The flies and parasites that torment sheep can be found in fear, tension, worry, uncertainty and the unknown for humans. Panic, discontent, agitation and restlessness do not have to conquer me. I am going to put his provisions into action. The Scripture says, "Be still and know that I am God." (Psalm 46:10). I have to learn to be quiet. Quietness for some is a way of life. It can be a time to reflect, a time to create, a time to recover, a time to grieve, a time to rejoice or a time to listen to God. I have to put aside the barriers, schedules, outside interruptions and intrusions. Spiritual intimacy is a must. I think activities and the busyness of life have caused me to get off the right track at times. I have to close my eyes and lay down in the green pastures. As I lay down, I reflect in the fact that God the Father chose me in Christ before the foundations of the world (Ephesians 1:4). He predestined me to be adopted as his own (v5). I reflect on the fact that God the Son carried out God's plan of redemption by shedding his blood on the cross. He redeemed me through his blood and provided forgiveness for my sins (v7). I reflect on the fact that God the Spirit will enable me to respond in faith to God's love and has guaranteed my inheritance (v 13,14). This reflecting brings peace and security. This will help bring freedom from the unknown.

God says, "wait on me – I will renew your strength, don't run and be weary, don't faint but walk in the Spirit" (Isaiah 40:31). I know that God will be with me. He is alive and present whether I feel his presence or not. He will not abandon me. He says "wait on me." I have to rely on him and look to him for my source of strength. Psalm 23 provides what I need to succeed. I do not have to carry the burden of the unknown. God says, give me your burdens, tell me about them, give me your worries and concerns. When I do, I am like the eagle (Isaiah 40:31). As he floats effortlessly in the wind, I can do the same because the unknown is placed into God's hands.

I am able to experience rest as I reflect upon the God in whom I believe. I must affirm daily that:

- I believe in one and only one God and that he is a personal and perfect Spirit who is infinite.
- I believe his attributes describe him and that he is sovereign.
- I believe he will provide rest in the green pasture because he cares.
- I believe in one God who is a trinity and is co-equal, God the Father, God the Son and God the Holy Spirit, and all three are present with me.
- I believe that God has a plan for all creation and is carrying out that plan. He will provide strength for my part.
- I believe there are no surprises with God. He is carrying out his will through providence.
- I believe that Jesus, begotten by the Holy Spirit, is truly God and man.

- I believe that Jesus voluntarily accepted his Father's will and came to earth in humanity, lived a perfect life as the sacrificial lamb to take upon himself my sin.
- I believe that Jesus' atonement is the way to my acceptance by God and also the defeat of Satan.
- I believe that Jesus' death totally accomplished the ransom for my sin.
- I believe in Jesus' literal physical resurrection. His resurrection guarantees mine. Believing in Jesus assures God's rest for me.
- I believe that the Holy Spirit is involved in all the acts of God.
- I believe that the Holy Spirit was sent to comfort me and give me rest.
- I believe the Holy Spirit is responsible for my regeneration and transformation.
- I believe the Holy Spirit indwells me and illuminates the Scripture to me.
- I believe that through the Holy Spirit I am able to affirm these facts that will provide rest for my spirit, soul and body.

As I learn to be in a resting mode, my mind and heart will hold onto the truth of God's Word. My thirst is quenched through his Word. As I allow it to saturate my mind, my soul becomes relaxed with his presence. His thoughts take control of my spirit. It starts with my spirit, then enters my soul and finally takes charge of my body. I have to learn to disallow the pollution of evil to enter my mind as I drink. The Scriptures will become my measuring rod to test everything. My quiet time becomes a restful, reflective and refueling experience. As I drink of the cool waters, it gives refreshing nourishment. I am putting his provisions into action. I can handle unknown issues in my life because God is equipping me through the Holy Spirit.

I am obtaining rest through recognition that God is giving the rest and a sense of well-being. As I affirm who he is and that he is in me, he produces the rest. I will follow him beside the quiet waters. I am not going to drink the dirty water that surrounds or creeps into the back door of my mind, but the pure water that flows from his Word. My thirst will be quenched because the Holy Spirit is doing the leading. I live in a confused and sick society. Christ comes quietly and invites me to come to him. He knows my heart, personality and soul. He has the capacity to satisfy. Only the Spirit and life of Christ himself will make me complete.

As my body needs water to stay alive, it also needs the indwelling of the Holy Spirit (I Corinthians 6:19) to quench my thirst. I cannot see him but his personality and presence are facts. His personality is proved in John 16:13,14. The pronoun "He" is used eight times to refer to the Holy Spirit. He is a real person because he comes, guides, hears, speaks, glorifies, receives and he shows.

It is hard to handle the unknown but with a counselor and helper like the Holy Spirit, I am able to succeed. To succeed, I have to follow his leadership by the quiet waters. When my heart is touched by him I have to respond. When his words make an impression in my mind, I must act. I have to practice repentance with honesty. I have to practice trust with loyalty. I have to practice obedience with love.

In my late teens, I wrote a little booklet entitled "A Touch of Heaven on Earth." I believe now, many years later, in the same things I wrote. If I want God's touch, I have to do what he wants. I have to learn daily to be sensitive to the Holy Spirit's presence. I have to stop resisting the Spirit. I have to stop saying no to his guidance. I have to stop refusing to yield to the Word of God as he brings it home to me. I have to be in a constant attitude of yieldedness rather than rebellion. I have to learn to stop sinning against the Spirit. I grieve the Holy Spirit when I break fellowship with him. Unconfessed sin has to be dealt with on a daily basis. I am not dealing with a force or power or influence, but with a person. The Bible says, "As ye have therefore received Christ Jesus the Lord, so walk ye in him." (Colossians 2:6). I received him by faith and the only way victory is obtained is in my dependence upon the Holy Spirit. He dwells in me and my heart has to be emptied of me and filled with him. The question is, Am I dominated by the Holy Spirit or by myself? Having a "touch of heaven" is through meeting certain conditions: stop resisting the Spirit, stop sinning against the Spirit, stop walking in the flesh.

Right at the time I think all is well, it seems everything will fall apart. The enemy knows my weaknesses. He certainly does not want me to bring glory to the Lord Jesus Christ. I cannot let my guard down. I have to realize that a battle is going on. At all times, I have to stand ready with offensive and defensive weapons.

I can face defeat. I can feel cast down. I can be distressed. I may be frustrated and experienced helplessness. I can even enter into depression. The struggles can be big in my eyes but not in God's eyes. I have to keep focused on him and when I take my eyes off of him, I will sink. Let's keep in mind that Jesus is a caring shepherd. In my spiritual dilemma, he doesn't become disgusted or fed up. I have experienced his love, compassion and tender care. He is ready to give reassurances, patience and restoration. In the path of life, there are many dangers. Restoration takes place when I am free of myself. God knows what he is doing with me. He is in charge. I am glad that he is ready to restore my soul.

I am glad God is ready to restore even when I have missed the mark. Sometimes I have forgotten that a battle is going on. As a musician-trumpeter, I have played "Sound the Battle Cry!" many times. Verse three says, "O Thou God of all, hear us when we call, help us one and all by thy grace; when the battle's done and the victory won, may we wear the crown before thy face." It seems suddenly in the midst of a calm, ordered and peaceful life, all the forces of Satan can break loose. He restores me through giving me understanding of the threefold attack. The act of creation is described as follows: "And the Lord God formed man of the dust of the ground and breathed into his nostrils the breath of life; and man became a living soul" (Genesis 2:7). The Scripture reveals that the body was made of the dust of the ground, that the spirit came from the breath of God and that the combination produced the soul (Hebrews 4:12). Satan's mind works against the spirit, soul and body of men. Against the body, he brings the temptations of the flesh. Against the soul, he brings the temptation of the world. Against the spirit, he comes himself or through one of his lesser agents.

I am not a casualty in the warfare. I can learn the subtle devices of the enemy, the devil. Let me begin with the flesh or body. I am not referring to the soft substance of the living body which covers the bones and is penetrated with blood. The body has a proper use of its every function and is normal, natural and moral. There is no sin involved or anything in connection with the human body itself. There is a human side apart from divine influence and it is prone to sin and oppose God. The body cannot run the affairs of the spirit and soul. It has to be controlled by the spirit and soul. When my will chooses to allow my body to dictate what it is going to do, then something is wrong. I am to abstain from anything that is in contrast to the principles of God's Word. I have to be so familiar with his Word that I will know what is right or wrong for me to do. It is not a bunch of rules but applied principles. Run from the enemy. The crucifixion of self has to take place. The enemy attacks the soul with the influence of the world. My senses are the focus. Whatever is drawing me away from the will of God is wrong to follow. If it keeps me away from Jesus, something is wrong. I cannot conform to the world's ideas. Conforming to the image of God's Son will show me what it means to not conform to the world.

Faith is the key word to build upon (I John 5:4), a definite turning away from the world "set eternity in the heart" (Ecclesiastes 3:11). Faith is a daily decision to respond to his Word in the correct way. The devil's greatest interest is my spirit. His desire is to keep me from God's guidance. The sins of the body and conformity to the world are terrible in themselves but the denial of God in the heart is unpardonable. Submission to God is absolutely necessary. Resisting comes next and putting on the armor of God will bring deliverance. In leaning on my own understanding (spirit-sin), I will fail to trust in the Lord with my whole heart (soul-sin) and will allow weakness in the body to flourish (flesh-sin). I am on the winning side with restoration bringing victory in the battle.

Like the sheep, I have to keep moving. I learned a long time ago (Isaiah 53:6) "All we like sheep have gone astray, we have turned everyone to his own way and the Lord hath laid on him the sin of us all." I like to go my own way but God knows what is the best way to go. Jesus said, "I am the way, the truth and the life" (John 14:6). Another favorite verse is found in Matthew 6:33, "Seek ye first the kingdom of God and his righteousness and all these things will be added unto you." I am like the sheep – blind, habitual and stupid. The little trails I follow become gullies. Turning to "my own way" simply means what I want. I have to learn to follow Jesus. He says, "If any man will follow me, let him deny himself daily and take up his cross and follow me" (Mark 8:34). I may at times give a mental assent to the idea but my will doesn't want to follow. This is the pivot point. The decision has to be made. "I will follow" means a rugged life of self-denial and attitude change. I have to deliberately put myself out on behalf of others. I have to be single-minded. I may have to stand alone. I have to learn to take a back seat. Self-determination has to change to dependence. Circumstances of life don't determine my attitude. Gratitude, peace and joy are seen in every situation.

Learning to cooperate with the Holy Spirit is the major focus. Right thinking will take place when my spirit and soul are in line with God's will. Learning to move on with his plan is necessary. He makes this possible by his own gracious Spirit who is given to those who obey (Acts 5:32). For it is he who works in us both to will and to do of his good pleasure (Philippians 2:13).

I think living righteously will produce correct thinking. My decisions have to be made with eternity in mind and his holiness. In verse three it says "path of righteousness" which is a pleasant and peaceful one because it is through God's name that provides his pure grace for the journey. I think following my own righteousness is worthless. It is built upon a self-achieved list of do's and don'ts. Righteous living and right-thinking involves:

- A relationship with God through belief in his Son.
- A realization that death with Christ and being raised with Christ brings newness of life.
- A recognition that God is doing the work on my behalf.
- A responsibility to get clean.
- A required cooperation with the Holy Spirit.
- A replacement of self-will for God's will.
- A removal of disobedience to daily obedience.
- A reminder to practice gratitude, peace and joy in every situation.

I have to adjust to God's thinking. Playing Christianity doesn't work. His path is full of responsibility and rewards.

There are many valleys I have crept through. I have learned to put the previous provisions into action. Now I can turn to the most intimate part of the Psalm – "the shadow of death." The sheep face dangers of rampaging rivers, avalanches, rock slides, poisonous plants and predators. I am fortunate to walk in the shadow of the Almighty. Jesus Christ has conquered death. I don't have to be air-lifted out of the situation. In every situation, in every dark trial, in every disappointment, in every distressing dilemma, I walk with the King. Every mountain has its valleys. The walk may be slow but it can be steady with Jesus. Intimate contact with Christ is the key. He says that he is with me. I have to learn to have an attitude of quiet acceptance of every adversity. Through the adversity, I can move to higher ground. My heart is full of thanksgiving when I realize God has given me a rod and staff to comfort me. The rod or club protects me. The rod becomes the extension of my arm. It is a symbol of strength, power and authority in any serious situation. The rod speaks of the Word of God. It implies the authority of Divinity. The staff provides care. The staff is a symbol of concern and compassion. It is an instrument of patience and kindness. The shepherd leans on it. It is a symbol of the Holy Spirit. The Holy Spirit will guide me, teach me, give understanding, give gentle promptings and counsel me. My reinforcement is provided through the Holy Spirit's constant presence and the use of Scripture against the enemy.

This power comes through his guidance, instruction, understanding, and gentle prompting. It is possible when I become intimate with Jesus Christ. Life can be complicated and cluttered. The Scripture calls for simplicity (Ecclesiastes 7:29). Cultivating intimacy with the Almighty will involve a changed life routine. In reading my spiritual autobiography, I discovered the necessity to stop. The triple career was exciting but too much. The decision was to simplify. Absolute silence has to follow the simplicity (Psalm 46:10). I have to make time for God. The picture is stillness, quietness, listening and waiting before him. This takes discipline but is indispensable if I hope to add depth to my spiritual life and be reinforced. There is no quick fix in becoming intimate with God. In my solitude, God does the examining (Psalm 139:1-4; 23-24). I have to do the confessing (I John 1:9). When I get rid of the complications of life, I am able to find a time for silence. In my silence, I am able to listen to God and make the adjustments. This will provide serenity in the soul. All these activities will bring me to complete trust (Proverbs 3:5,6). No longer am I preoccupied with working on the details in my life. Unqualified reliance in the living Lord takes place.

My life will have days of gladness and sadness. It will experience delightful days and dark days. I still have a great, sovereign, gracious and good shepherd who provides for me even in the midst of my enemies. He anoints my head with oil. He cares for the sheep and he cares for me. The overflowing presence of the Holy Spirit is continually overshadowing me. Coping with unknown issues turns into contentment when my conscious thought-life becomes anointed by the Holy Spirit. I can be free from the world's contamination through faith and acceptance. Just as I have asked Christ to come into my life initially, I need to invite the Holy Spirit to come into my mind to monitor my thought life.

God provides all the preparations to help me. He knows ahead of time my needs. I am blessed with the understanding that he is in charge (sovereignty). I am blessed with experiencing his goodness (grace). I am blessed with his love (mercy). I am blessed with his sufficiency (abundance). I am blessed with his resources (filling). These give me reassurance of his greatness, graciousness and goodness directed toward me.

As I learn to rely on God, his goodness and mercy will pursue me and I will always be at home with him. "I will never leave you nor forsake you" (Hebrews 15:5). I have a privileged position. No matter what comes, my treatment will be with goodness, mercy and his presence. I may have limited knowledge, understanding, wisdom and comprehension but I have an inner witness of the Holy Spirit. He provides confidence as I work through the provision of rest, refreshment, restoration, right-thinking, reinforcement, reassurance and reliance. No disaster, difficulty or dilemma will take charge of my spirit, soul and body. My serenity has its basis on a total reliance on God's ability to do the right thing and the best thing in any given situation for me. God's presence involves his promises.

Supernatural Power

Life becomes a celebration as I follow Jesus. It involves his supernatural power. This power is received through the development of God's thoughts saturating my thoughts (I Corinthians 2:11,12). The more I think upon God's Word, the more I will think like God. His view of things will become my views. His attitudes will become mine. Knowing God's will causes me to pray in his will. It is exciting to explore the vastness of an infinite God. It is also exciting to see how I am wonderfully made (Psalm 139:14). Through my situation, I am more conscious of how the heart and brain work. I also refer this to knowledge and experience. The situation and the knowledge of God must be transferred to the heart. The brain and heart oversee complex systems that are necessary for life, the nervous system and the circulatory system. Each is encased in a protective fortress of calcium, one inside the cranium and the other within the rib cage. They are on the job all the time with no days off until death or the resurrection day. The human brain is the single most complex apparatus of all God's vast creative genius. It is the center of my nervous sytem and contains billions of neurons, each having thousands of synoptic connections. The heart is smaller than my brain but no less impressive. In an average lifetime, the heart contracts and relaxes two and a half billion times without stopping to rest. At 72 beats a minute, that is over 4,000 beats an hour and over 100,000 beats every day. In every heart, blood is drawn into my heart, filtered, processed and pumped back out again to every millimeter of my body. The brain is the center of my thinking and the heart represents my affection, emotion and personality. I have to learn to love the Lord with all my heart (Mark 12:30) and to keep my heart with all diligence for out of it springs the issues of life (Proverbs 4:23). Sometimes it is hard to get the message from head to heart.

The knowledge of God has to filter down into the heart. It takes nourishment from God's Word through observation, interpretation and application. I have to inform my thinking through contemplation. I will then understand his perspectives. I am all set as I respond to the text, "What think ye of Christ" (Matthew 22:42). I am learning to be a doer of the Word (James 1:22). This is absolutely necessary for me. My heart stopped pumping blood as a matter of fact during surgery. A life machine kept it pumping. After four bypasses and some valve work, it started to work on its own again. The nervous system, the circulatory system, the rib cage and the emotions and personality have all been affected. I discovered that the supernatural power of God can be infused in me through the Holy Spirit. The saturating of God's word through accepting its authority, the applying it and studying it will make me think like God.

Read from my devotional book "Thoughts to Ponder," pgs 7-8. The Bible says, "And he reasoned in the synagogue and persuaded the

Jews and Greeks, and he continued teaching the Word of God among them" (Acts 18:4,11). I know of no other way to give the authority of the Scriptures than to continue teaching the word. I would like to reason and persuade you that the Scriptures ares a living, vital agency with supernatural power in itself. Read the promise, "For as the rain cometh down and the snow from heaven, and returneth not thither, but watereth the earth, and maketh it bring forth and bud, that it may give seed to the sower and bread to the eater; so shall my word be that goeth forth out of my mouth. It shall not return unto me void, but it shall accomplish that which I please, and it shall prosper in the thing whereto I sent it" (Isaiah 55:10,11). To the same purpose Jeremiah has written: "Is not my word like as a fire? saith the Lord; and like a hammer that breaketh the rock in pieces?" (Jeremiah 23:29). God uses his word,

"For the word of God is quick and powerful and sharper than any two-edged sword, piercing even to the dividing asunder of soul and spirit, and of the joints and marrow, and is a discerner of the thoughts and intents of the heart" (Hebrews 4:12).

The Bible is an ancient book for modern times. It is one book, one history and one story; one mind produced it. God himself became a man so that we might know what to think when we think of God. I could give all the evidences for scriptural authority but why don't you read the Bible for yourself and let it prove itself?

The Bible says, "As newborn babes, desire the sincere milk of the word, that ye may grow thereby" (I Peter 2:2). God has given his word so that believers may grow thereby. We haven't fulfilled our obligations to the word until application has taken place. The Bible is not only the source book for information but has life changing power for today. Growth in the spiritual life comes not merely from hearing but from hearing and doing. The Bible says, "the effectual doer shall be blessed in what he does" (James 1:25). "If you know these things, you are blessed if ye do them" (John 12:17).

The Bible has been given so that man's basic nature can be changed. "All scripture is given by God and is profitable for teaching, for reproof, for correction, for training in righteousness, that the man of God may be adequate, equipped for every good work" (2 Timothy 3:16,17). It teaches, rebukes, restores, trains for righteous living. It equips us to do the work that God wants us to do. The Bible convicts, regenerates, nurtures, cleanses, counsels, guides, prevents sin, revives, strengthens, gives wisdom, delivers and helps. The Bible alone realistically and sufficiently meets man's deepest problems, longings, needs and inadequacies. It provides the answers to man's needs for deliverance from the penalty of sin, for spiritual progress for victory, for guidance and for personal relationships and conduct. As we learn the Scriptures, let us apply it to our daily activities.

The Bible says, "Blessed are the undefiled in the way, who walk in the law of the Lord" (Psalm 119:1). What is wrong with reading the Bible? Why do people think it so strange? Some people have the idea that the Bible is just for the mentally weak, some people think it is for the ignorant, some people imagine that it is just for the shut-ins and some think it is only for the children. Why do the teens and young adults turn from it? I believe they do not go on to read it or believe it or study it or follow it. If we are going to walk in the law of the Lord, we must follow this pattern.

We need to study it through, that is, master a verse every day. Think of it and at the end of the year, you will have 365 verses in your heart and in your mind to bring about happiness, direction, peace and contentment. We need to pray about it. We must let each verse become a part of our very being, praying the verse into reality and then seeing the promises of God, as we claim them, change our lives. We must write down our thoughts. We cannot remember everything but our computer mind has it and we need to refresh our memory. That, of course, brings us to working it out. Let the Bible get in your heart and then live it out every day. It is not good only to study it through or pray about it or put it down or work it out, but we must also pass it on. We must talk about it. Let the word of God inspire and bless your heart. This takes discipline.

You cannot be lazy. Walk in the law of the Lord and you will find purpose and peace. As I learn to follow Jesus, life will become a celebration because it involves his supernatural power.

The Promise of Peace

As I look at myself, my family, community, state and country, I am thankful that "God is our refuge and strength." Come with me and learn to be still and know that he is God (Psalm 46:8,10). This Psalm is a song of deliverance. It is a hymn of praise and an expression of confidence. I hope as you read what I have learned that it will make sense to you and bring peace when in fear.

Read his words, "God is our refuge and strength, a very present help in trouble" (v 1). I am in a safe position. I don't have to get burdened down with the troubles around me or in me because my helper is God. The question to ask is 'who is in charge?' I don't have to fear because God says, 'fear not.' When I am fearful, I read this Psalm over and over again to obtain rest and peace, and it works. No violent disturbances that I may encounter will create fear but rather a calm spirit. I can do anything that is in God's will because he indwells me. I have confidence in him when he says, "I will help you" (v 4-5). God's grace is at work bringing victory. Since the Garden of Eden, God has always had a river to bring peace. "The heathen raged, the earth melted… God is my refuge" (v 6-7). I realize that trouble can come from outward or inward influences. It is everywhere and beyond my comprehension. God has promised to deliver the righteous. He will defeat the enemy no matter how big or strong. He will completely devastate them. The offensive weapons of the enemy are no match for God. I am learning to "be still and know that God is God" (v 10). When I have a problem with no solution or situation that turns bad, I know God will work it out for my good and his glory. Let's stand back and watch intently the mighty hand of God. It is not easy, it takes work, it takes training and it takes a spirit that is willing. As I pursue the correct thinking in regard to fear, I find much strength in these words:

- He is with me
- Know that I am God
- Behold his work
- God shall help
- He is my refuge and strength (Psalm 46)

Reflect back into history to Exodus 15. I have found the same truth in Psalm 46. It says that redemption by blood was followed by redemption by power. This is the first recorded song in the Bible. God has carried his blood-redeemed people through the Red Sea. Trusting in the Lord brings deliverance. He will help and his timing is perfect. Uncertainties, sorrow, weeping and tribulation will come. Trust, wait and rejoice because a new day is promised and the trouble will melt in his presence (Psalm 46:4-7). Universal peace will come and the Prince of the world and god of this age will be defeated (Psalm 46:8-11). The once rejected light and life, the creator, the Son of God and my Savior will be exalted. At this point, I should sing 'A Mighty Fortress Is Our God.' Jesus Christ is my refuge and strength.

I am concerned with the phrase, "therefore, will not we fear" (Psalm 46:2,3). Fear is anxiety caused by approaching danger, the unknown and troublesome times. I have learned in these times to seek, love and trust. How do I put this into action? I decided to accept Matthew 6:33 as a promise to rely upon. It is a summary of Jesus' Sermon on the Mount. He says to continue seeking and to be constant in the endeavor. I should have one dominant concern. His kingdom should be my spiritual priority. My fears will diminish as I seek him. He has promised that my material needs will be taken care of. He adds to this thought to keep thinking upon today, not tomorrow. A growing relationship with the Son of God is necessary (John 1:12). This provides the Holy Spirit's residence in me. My body, soul and spirit will begin to find rest through seeking intently.

After seeking is in progress, I discovered that God has given me power, love and a sound mind (2 Timothy 1:7). I have access to supernatural resources that will provide self-control (a sound mind). Fear will not produce weakness with a mind that is disciplined. I think the word 'fear' should be replaced with the word 'love.' Love has greater strength than fear. It has the ability to establish confidence and endurance. When fears enter my emotional nature, I have to reject it and replace it with love. The Bible says, "there is no fear in love but love drives out fear" (1 John 4:18,19). I have to anticipate and plan in ways that no longer center upon myself and my fears and concerns. I have to dominate my life with love. Love requires loving "the Lord with all your heart and with all your soul and with all your mind" (Matthew 22:37). This means that I have to give total love. It is a love which directs my thoughts and actions. Fear looks at evil, consequences, suspicions and worry, but love looks at opportunity, belief and goodness.

As I seek intently and as I love with determination, I will find myself in his care (1 Peter 5:6,7). God says "Humble yourself, therefore, under God's mighty hand that he may lift you up in due time. Cast all your anxiety-fear on him because he cares for you" (1 Peter 5:7-11). Psalm 46 and 1 Peter 5 go hand in hand. He is my refuge and strength and he holds my destiny in his hands. I know that God cares because I have been seeking him. I can live with serenity in God because God's love has replaced my fear. This text will provide confidence, assurance, acceptance and certainty. As I cast my care upon God, I will be committed to trust. I will wait for his response. I will rely upon his restoration. The hymn found in Psalm 46 will wash fear from my veins. Love is greater than the enemy. His promise of deliverance will be fulfilled. God is my refuge and strength—Come and see the works of God—Be still and know that I am God (Psalm 46:1,8,10).

The Promise of Victory

My prayer is "cause me to hear thy lovingkindness…for in thee do I trust, cause me to know the way wherein I should walk; for I lift up my soul unto thee, deliver me" (Psalm 143:7-9). I have asked God to do it. I cannot do it on my own. I have a willing heart but am weak. My hope is fixed in the promises of God. He is faithful and he will bring deliverance. The fullest meaning of his faithfulness is found in the cross and the finished work of the Son of God. The reception of Jesus is the beginning of life (John 1:12; 14:6).

As I have traveled in this new life, I have experienced many trials. I am going to share some insight from the Old Testament (Psalm 40:1-17) and the New Testament (1 Corinthians 10:13) to compare what they have to say. It has helped me be assured of victory. In the New Testament it says, "There hath no temptation taken you." The words here can mean a trial which takes many forms like hatred, hunger, sleeplessness, pain, misunderstanding, worry and discouragement. It can mean testing which can help me grow in grace. It can also mean a temptation which is what Satan uses to weaken me. How I handle temptation is dependent on what I think and how I act and react. In Psalm 40:2, it says "he brought me up also out of a horrible pit." Sometimes I have experienced a deep sense of agony. It seems the trial has brought me to the bottom. Through Christ's humility and my substitute on the cross, he has delivered me from the pit through his death and resurrection. The overwhelming infirmities are no match to the mighty grace of God. The word 'many' in verse 5 reveals his marvelous works (Ephesian 2:7). In humility I have started on the path to victory.

Back to 1 Corinthians 10:13 where it says, "no temptation has seized you but such is common to man," I am reminded that I am not alone in this pain. My situation is not unique. God's promise is to help me in any situation. In Psalm 40:2, God refers to the 'miry clay' which reminds me of a thousand ways that I can be tempted and tested. I have found myself at times in a big mess but I am not alone because God is faithful. God knows all about me. He is fully aware of my problems. In this verse, God says he will not permit me to be tempted above that I am able. I am confident that I will not be tested beyond my capacity to endure. If I keep this truth in mind, my attitude and behavior will follow the right course. I have waited patiently for the Lord. "Blessed is the man who makes the Lord his trust" (v 1,4). Patience and waiting united will produce faith.

Faith is a decision to rely upon God's promises. God will provide during the trial a way to safety. In Psalm 40:1, it says that "God inclined unto me." This word contains the idea of bowing down. It is a fitting picture of the grace of God. The sinner is in the pit and crying out and God bows down to meet the need. The Lord bowed all the way down until he met me at the bottom of the pit. Now, through his resurrection, I bow down to him and receive victory. In 1 Corinthians 10:13, it says 'ye may be able to bear it." I can overcome my struggles by having my mind focused on the truth. He will set my feet on a solid rock and will establish my goings. He will give a new song and will reveal my testing to others. He will participate with me in victory. Now, pray the prayer, "cause me to hear…deliver me" (Psalm 143:7,8). Read Psalm 40:1-17 slowly and recite 1 Corinthians 10:13 between each verse. I have discovered in humility assurance of victory through this process. "Blessed is the man who maketh the Lord his trust" (Psalm 40:4).

The Promise of Hope

Sometimes life is cruel, sometimes it is full of suffering, physically and psychologically, sometimes our life expectations fail, sometimes there is little meaning to life, sometimes there is desperation and despair and sometimes there is just a falling out in the realities of life. Hope in the scripture always is a confident expectation. The word carries with it no uncertainties. I can be sure of the faithfulness of God in fulfilling his promises. With hope I have conviction and assurance.

- People with longstanding problems need hope
- People with peculiarly difficult problems need hope
- People that have been misled in regard to their problems need hope

- People who are harassed by fear need hope
- People whose hopes have been dashed repeatedly need hope
- People that have tried and failed need hope
- People that have dramatic changes in life need hope
- People that have fallen into depression need hope
- People who have suffered life shattering experiences need hope

When I find myself searching for help, I find it in the hope that I have in Jesus. I have learned through Psalm 39:1-13 my innermost thoughts toward the wicked should be confident and not complaining. I should not embarrass God with my tongue (v 1-2). My innermost thoughts toward God should be honest and not with a bitter attitude. I must share my anguish and pain (v 3-4). When I am searching for hope, my innermost thoughts toward myself should not be deceived. I have to learn God's perspective on life (v 5-6). My innermost thoughts toward deliverance should be scripture-directed (v 7-13).

I have learned that in despair, I can experience confidence (v 7). I have learned that in confession that I can be released (v 8). I have learned that correction is needed sometimes (v 9-11). I have also been comforted (v 12-13). These thoughts have started the path to hope.

I am discovering with excitement that in Jesus Christ's name, I can live with hope and obtain the help I need. He is worth believing. There is no one whose understanding of life has come close to his. Jesus is in the life-changing business. All kinds of people have come to him: satisfied people, messed up people, sick and injured people, forgotten people, despised people, admired people, worthy people and religious people. I have come to him. Jesus has been changing lives for two thousand years. I am learning to leap out of my skin into faith. It is a realization of less of me and more of him. Not only do I have to let go of self and replace self with him, but I have to learn to wait. This is the in-between period. When I hold onto his promise, "my hope is in Jesus...hear my prayer, O

Lord, listen to my cry for help" (Psalm 39:7,12). I know victory will come because he keeps to his word. Some adjustments have to be made during the waiting time for victory. As I apply the attributes of God to the names given to Jesus, I will be given help and hope.

His name is wonderful (Isaiah 9:6). I believe in an awesome God. He can make my life wonderful because he is wonderful. My first adjustment in obtaining help is believing that he is awesome. Wonderful things have happened, are happening and will continue to happen. It all starts with experiencing forgiveness of sin and the invasion of a whole new life. "Christ liveth in me" (Galatians 2:20). Believing in Jesus is required (Acts 16:31). He wants intimate fellowship. "I count all things to be loss in view of the surpassing value of knowing Christ Jesus my Lord" (Philippians 3:7,8). Knowing God is the most important thing I can accomplish. My goal is to know him so well that I can say "I have received a spirit of adoption as sons by which I cry, 'Abba, Father!' The word 'abba' is equivalent to 'daddy'. It is a term of respect and endearment.

By knowing God, I can better understand how I am to live. As I contemplate God's attributes through his names, I have been promised strength, encouragement and help. I know God loves me. God is love and the one who abides in love abides in God and God abides in him (1 John 4:16). I am surrounded with his infinite person, power and glory (John 14:20). "And I will pray the Father, and ye in me and I in you" (v 16,20). He is more than with me, he is in me. He indwells in me. He also supplies in himself all that any soul will ever need in time or eternity. The union I have in Christ is beyond my comprehension. The oneness that I have with Jesus means many things (John 17:20-23). My emphasis here is fellowship. It is awesome to say that I have an everlasting companionship with him in the place we live. I am looking for the eternal security which starts here and now as I draw near to him. 'To be in Christ' refers to my position-union with Christ. In believing, I have that relationship and possession of the divine. I am safe in his hands because I am associated with the creator-redeemer God.

His name is counselor. I believe in an all-knowing God. He is my counselor and knows everything. "Who has directed the Spirit of the Lord or as his counselor has informed him? With whom did he consult and gave him understanding? And who taught him in the path of justice and taught him knowledge, and informed him of the way of understanding?" (Isaiah 40:13,14). God knows what he knows simply because he knows it. He did not learn it. The second adjustment is to accept his counsel. He is qualified to counsel me. He is eternal God whom "dwelleth all the fullness of the Godhead bodily" (Colossians 2:9). Jesus Christ was a part of the eternal counsel of creation. He was there when the Father said, "let us make man." He understands me because he became man. He is able to enter into the experiences that perplex and burden me. He knows my heart and mind and is able to help me understand myself. I have to let go of myself and let him take over. I must sit back and learn to watch him work. He knows me, my feelings, desires and my personality and disease. He has known everything from the beginning. Nothing can escape his all-encompassing knowledge. I have learned that God permits trials for reasons we may or may not understand, but he is able to bring good out of even the worst circumstances. I am able to have confidence because he knows all the possibilities. He is personal. He knows my thought process. God is concerned about the details as he knows everything going on behind the scenes (Job 23:10).

His name is mighty God. I believe in a powerful God. Jesus is God himself. There is nothing that God cannot do. His unlimited power will reflect his divine glory and accomplish his sovereign will. He is able to "call into being that which does not exist" (Romans 4:17). Nothing is impossible with God. The scripture says, "thou has formed my inward parts...I am fearfully and wonderfully made" (Psalm 139:13,14). God's power is very personal. He is able to deliver and is able to keep me standing in his presence. He says be strong in the Lord and in the strength of his might (Ephesians 6:10). The third adjustment for change is the fact that he is mighty God. He is called "Immanuel" God with us. I have to understand his claims and accept his deity. With that response, I am strengthened with all might. He takes care of the demands of life. No matter what the problem, he has power to meet it, handle it, solve it and use it for my good and his glory

His name is everlasting Father. I believe in a sovereign God. He is the originator of eternity. I live in a new dimension of life. God has absolute rule and control over all of his creation. God rules absolutely over the affairs of men. God can do whatever he wants to do simply because it is all his. Everything that occurs does so under the hand of a sovereign God. The fourth adjustment for change is in his name, the everlasting Father. God has created me for eternity and Jesus Christ came to earth to reveal eternity (I John 1:1,2). There is more to life than what my senses reveal. In trusting Jesus, I am able to meet every detail of life with confidence. I am safe in Jesus because of who he is. I exist for him. I can live in confidence because Jesus provides strength. There are no chance happenings. Whatever happens, it will bring good (Psalm 8:28). He has the whole picture. I can trust in Jesus and he is able to guard what I have entrusted to him.

His name is Prince of Peace. I believe in an intimate God. The fifth adjustment for change is peace. When I accomplish the alignment process through his grace, I will experience peace. Jesus brings peace because he is peace. Do not try to change the circumstances but change in character. Peace does not come from the outside in but in reality comes from the inside out. I am learning that my testing, trials and temptations can become a win-win situation. I must learn to let go of self. I must learn to make the adjustments. I must learn to practice the victory in peace. He is free from limitations of space. He is everywhere present. He is in me. I believe in an awesome God because he is wonderful in all his acts. He wants fellowship with me. I believe in an all-knowing God because he provides wise counsel. He has all knowledge and knows my inner needs. I believe in a powerful God because there is nothing he cannot do. I believe in a sovereign God because he is the originator of eternity. He is in control. When I reflect upon these facts and allow them to penetrate my spirit, soul and body, I am able to face today.

As I repeat the names of Jesus with a sincere heart and allow the Holy Spirit to enable me, I will be encouraged. This is a starting point. Authentic transformation takes time. It is a process and is not a formula to follow. It is not some basic principles to apply. It is not a mechanical determination. It is faith working in me through the Holy Spirit's guidance and power. "May the God of hope fill you with all joy and peace as you trust in him, so that you may overflow with hope by the power of the Holy Spirit" (Romans 15:13).

The promise of hope is provided through Jesus. I am thankful for the Lord's presence. This chapter was written when I started a new journey in my life. I am facing a fearful, dreadful uncertainty in my health. The biopsy has returned with a positive result. Cancer is the disease. I was told that my cancer is the second killer of man. That information was really encouraging. I am waiting for the details and what treatment options I have. I can list some of them but do not like the side effects. I still need to know the facts. The initial shock has started to wear off. My family is very supportive. I know their prayers and spiritual perspective will continue to be helpful.

My daughter shared a prayer and Psalm 91:11, "He who dwells in the shelter of the most High will rest in the shadow of the Almighty." She has started a network of prayer support. My son immediately gave me a verse from Hosea 6:3 "Let us acknowledge the Lord…as surely as the sun rises he will appear…he will come to us." He has set up a network of prayer warriors. I am so pleased that they have accepted this challenge in the way they have. They know what works and they know what pleases God. Both Bible references, without them knowing it, reinforce the verse the Holy Spirit gave to me and my wife, James 4:8, "Draw near to God and he will draw near to you." My dark thoughts have turned to the light because Jesus is wonderful. My folly has turned to wise thinking because Jesus is my counselor. Losing heart has changed to a conquering spirit because Jesus is my mighty God. I have been drawing closer to my everlasting Father who holds eternity in his hands. When I think of these names of Jesus, peace from the Prince of Peace has entered my spirit. "Jesus is the sweetest name I know, and he's just the same as his lovely name, and that's the reason why I love him so, O Jesus is the sweetest name I know."

Assignment: Encouraging Activities

To change feelings, we must change thinking. Inaction will bring misery. Learn to apply the Scripture to your life. The result will bring strength, support and steadfastness.

Affirm God's Intervention

1. Read the leaflet (one section at a time) with the expectation that it will work.
2. As you review the text, receive what is says.
3. Adapt each phrase into your personal prayer.
4. Test the results: Does it work to change your thought patterns?
5. Do you have confidence in God's Word?

Accept God's Indwelling
1. Have you responded to God's invitation?
2. How do you come to Jesus?
3. Have you made the necessary decisions?
4. What is the difference between accepting and receiving Christ?
5. What is the definition of faith?

Adjust to God's Illumination
1. Confess your weakness
2. Ask for supernatural power.
3. Practice the fruit
4. Experience God's presence.
5. Is your spirit at rest?

I have been able to follow God's plan of action in my life through practicing his promises. This scripture, Psalm 100:3, has proven to be profitable. Read the examples given to bring comfort. Affirm his intervention and experience victory. Adjust to God's illumination with hope.

About the Author:

John F. Gillette's story begins and ends with a song he sang in his childhood: "His Very Own:"

> "His very own, His very own,
> Wonderful Grace in His Word is made known,
> chosen by the Father,
> purchased by the Son,
> sealed by the Spirit,
> I am his very own."

His desire every day is to glorify the Lord Jesus Christ in health and in sickness. He has learned every moment needs to be in God's presence.

Divine dialogue is a developmental process. He has been a lifelong student of the Scriptures. It is easy to fail the standards of God but he has an inner passion that he calls "the holy urge" to encourage him to go forward. His studies have been in the liberal arts but always guided through his biblical deep-rooted foundation. His graduate research has been in religion and leadership.

He has served Jesus Christ since his childhood with diversity, independence and confidence in education, pastorate and leadership. His pastoral health care discovery series was published to help himself and minister to others who are having struggles in making spiritual, psychological and physiological adjustments.

More Books in the Series:

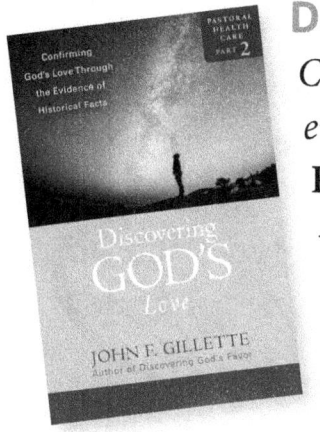

Discovering God's Love
Confirming God's love through the evidence of historical facts
Pastoral Health Care—Part Two

We can obtain strength to conquer through a knowledge of the 'Gospels' and receiving Jesus Christ into our hearts. The New Testament books of history give evidence of God's love. Through his love and faith, we are able to be strengthened, experience his support and become steadfast.

Discovering God's Counsel
Applying his spiritual solution to meet difficult trials
Pastoral Health Care—Part Three

Dark days can be life threatening. We have to develop an adequate level of spiritual, psychological and physiological adjustments. We can live with confidence in God's sufficiency.

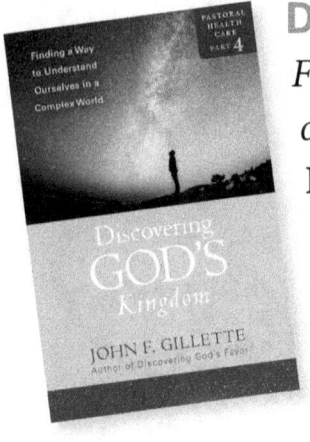

Discovering God's Kingdom
Finding a way to understand ourselves in a complex world
Pastoral Health Care—Part Four

Dealing with life, death, heaven and eternity with God's perspective is necessary. It involves a personal decision of belief, trust and faith. Knowledge and commitment will bring comfort and security. The eternal destiny directive will provide the way.

Discovering God's Heart
Feeling God's heart pulse is our daily challenge
Pastoral Health Care—Part Five

We have to practice the principles in the pastoral health care meditation method. We can handle any situation through thinking biblically. The spirit, soul and body are involved. Therefore, a holistic approach has to take place.

www.ingramcontent.com/pod-product-compliance
Lightning Source LLC
Chambersburg PA
CBHW070115080526
44586CB00013B/1304